# Honour
## God's Master Key to the Blessing

Author
Clint Ross

Honour God's Master Key to the Blessing

First published 2018



Editing done by Bonita Solomons and Claudine Erasmus
Book cover and graphic designs done by Sadé Stoffberg and Antonio Erasmus

ISBN:  978 0620 79452 7

## ACKNOWLEDGEMENTS

It gives me great joy to firstly honour my parents, Clarence and Leonie Ross, who taught me honour without always using the right terms when explaining it … for instance, how to speak and respond to those older or in authority to me.

Then there are the pastors under whom I served and I especially want to honour Pastor Albert Wiggins from Logos Assembly of God. I learnt so much from him about being a minister with integrity and honour.

Pastor Chris Ross, my biological brother has mentored me over the years. His leadership and wisdom has helped me to access great doors.

Dr Mike Murdock, the man whose teachings have transformed my world. I would not have been where I am in life, had it not been for the teachings of the man I call "Dad" today. His wisdom teachings have placed everything into perspective. Most of my learning on the topic of honour I have learnt from his teachings, hence I will quote him throughout this book.

Pastor Ana Sweet, who is a daughter in the Lord of Dr Murdock. I have learnt much from her on this topic and appreciate our one on one talks and her teaching material she has shared with me.

To the most caring and loving person, Chantal my wife, who believes in me more than I believe in myself. She is a true example of living an honourable life and I learn so much from her every day.

My two precious children Lee-Ann and Kyle, who has embraced this teaching in their daily lives. They inspire me to keep learning and teaching.

Then to the one who gave me life itself, the precious Holy Spirit. Jesus said that He is the one who will teach us in all truth. In my prayers, I asked the Holy Spirit to teach me honour. My life changed drastically after that, as He opened my eyes to the truth in His Word and my environment. Not

everything that I will share came from my
mentors and books, some of the revelations
came directly from the Holy Spirit. I am
honoured that He would teach me... He is
my greatest teacher.

**WHY I WROTE THIS BOOK**

**Proverbs 10v22. The blessing of the Lord maketh rich, and he addeth no sorrow with it.**

For many years I have desired to taste of the blessing of the Lord and have always been intrigued by successful people and how they've achieved their success. Especially those who has accredited their success to living for God.

For more than 18 years, I have been a great admirer of Dr Mike Murdock. I have read most of his books and listened to many of his tapes and cd's.

My life was greatly impacted, by a statement he made when I met him in his office at the Wisdom Center in Fort Worth Texas.

He looked me in the eyes and said "son,

**Honour Will Take You Further Than Your Faith.**

**Honour Will Take You Further Than Your Genius.**

**Honour Will Take You Further Than Your Education."**

Those words hit me so hard and I just knew that he had given me a key that would change my life.

A year prior that, I was having coffee with Prophet Marius Higgins, a well-known prophet in South Africa. He prophesied over me and said, God will give me keys that I will give people to unlock doors for them, but He will give me a master key that will unlock every door.

After being with Dr Murdock in Texas I came home desiring to understand more on the subject of honour.  I would love to share my findings in this book, as I have discovered the master key to every door that Prophet Marius Higgins spoke about...**The key of Honour**

If you will learn and embrace the teachings in this book, I guarantee you that your life and those whom you influence will never be the same again.

I am excited for you and your generations, as the master key to your success has just been handed to you.

I am also not for one moment saying that I know everything on this subject, as I believe there is so much more to the subject of **Honour** that I'm still learning.

I love things to be explained to me in a simple and logical way, so I'll do my best to do the same in this book.

There are various definitions of honour:
- High respect,
- Great esteem,
- To make glorious,
- To cause the dignity and worth of someone to be acknowledged, etc

My purpose with this book is to give you an understanding of honour and practical applications that will help you in your daily walk.

*The anointing is caught, but honour is taught...*

I pray you will take on the posture of a learner as you read this book. Through learning you will do well. **Isaiah 1v17** says," **Learn to do well..."**

*Everyone wants to do well, but not everyone wants to learn.*

Your success and that of your generations are important to me ... that's why I wrote this book.

# CHAPTER 1

## WHERE DOES HONOUR COME FROM

### Heaven Is A Place of Honour

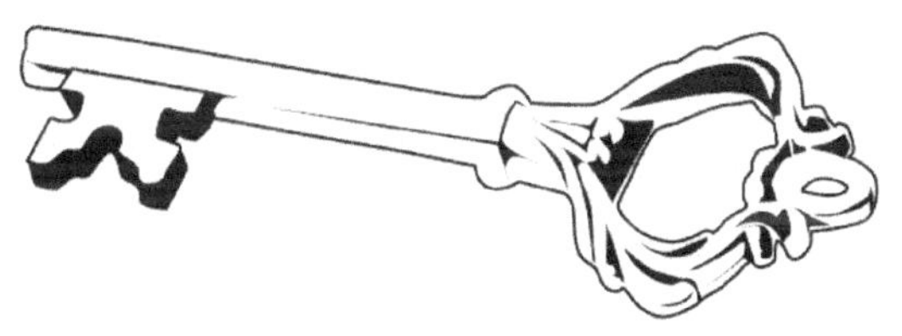

Wisdom key:

God dwells in an

environment of honour

- Ps Clint Ross

**Heaven Is A Place of Honour.**

Honour has its origin in God...

**And when those beasts give GLORY and HONOUR and thanks to him that sat on the throne, who liveth for ever and ever, The four and twenty elders fall down before him that sat on the throne, and worship him that liveth for ever and ever, and cast their crowns before the throne, saying, Thou art worthy, O Lord, to receive Glory and Honour and Power: for thou has created all things, and for thy pleasure they are and were created.  (Revelation 4v9-11).**

In the fourth chapter of Revelation, John describes what he sees in heaven. The atmosphere of heaven is filled with Glory and Honour. It is the fragrance of heaven. Continuous Worship in heaven creates continuous Glory in heaven...Continuous Order in heaven creates continuous Honour in heaven... God will not share His glory with mankind, but He has decided to share honour with them. God shares His glory

with no man... **I am the Lord: that is my name: and my glory will I not give to another... (Isaiah 42v8).**
God however, shares honour with mankind... **Honour all men. Love the brotherhood. Fear God. Honour the King. (1 Peter 2v17).**
Godly honour flows from a place of love and not man made fear. The fear referred to in this scripture, is a godly reverence. When honour is forced upon through fear, resentment will follow. Many admire the gangs for their code of honour, but that is kept out of fear and not love. Anything that flows from fear, is not of God. Godly honour flows from a heart of love.
**Proverbs 29v25 The fear of man brings a snare...**
Glory we give to God only...
Honour we give to God and man...
The bible teaches us that we are made in the image of God and have been designed for glory and honour.

**For thou has made him a little lower than the angels, and hast crowned him with glory and honour.  (Psalms 8v5).**

God will not share His glory with man because it's connected to worship... when we worship God, He manifests His glory....

**..for thou shall worship no other god: for the Lord, whose name is Jealous, is a jealous God. (Exodus 34v14).**

Moses came from the mountain and his face shone from the glory of God, but God never allowed the children of Israel to worship him, but He did expect of them to honour him. **Exodus 34** There is a song we sing that says, "**All Honour, All Glory, All Power Belongs to You.**" The scripture in **Revelation 4v11** does not say **All.** It says," **Thou art worthy, O Lord, to receive glory and honour and power...**"
The word **All** in the song has confused some good, God-fearing people, who thinks that honouring man is wrong because they believe that God alone deserves honour, but the bible teaches us differently. The bible is full of examples of people who honoured other people, and God was very pleased. God wants us as his people, to learn how to give and receive honour.

Giving honour is great, but we must also learn how to receive it. It takes humility to do both. One of the young men in our church came to me before a service one day and asked if he could carry my bible, something I have done for many other men and women. My response to him was, "Do you think there is something wrong with my hands?" As he walked away, the Holy Spirit said to me, "You are humble enough to give honour, but you are too full of pride to receive it." I have just stopped the flow of honour in this young man towards me as his pastor. How can I expect him to honour me in other ways, if I am the one blocking the pipeline of honour from him to me? I immediately called him back and said it was okay for him to do it. It is not just good enough for you to learn how to give honour, you must also learn how to receive it. In heaven, there is a constant giving and receiving of honour. When you enter what I call "the world of honour," you live to give and receive honour all the time.

# CHAPTER 2

## THE EARTH IS FILLED WITH DISHONOUR

**God Has an Order**
**The Good News**
**Honour Has Rewards**

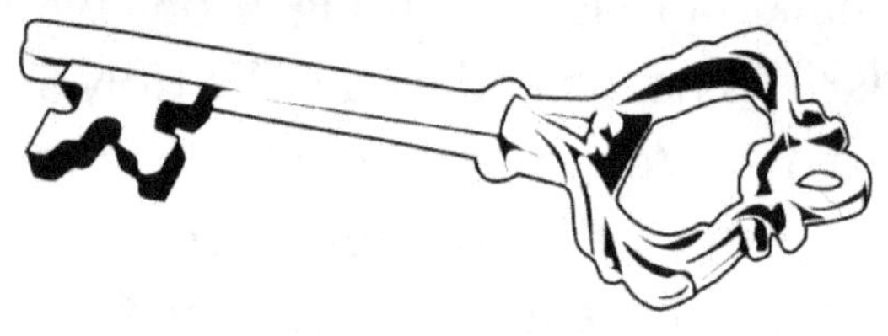

Wisdom key:

The devil does not want you to learn how

to demonstrate honour...

Because he knows it's a key to your door

of blessing

- Ps Clint Ross

Dishonour has its origin in the devil.

**And the earth was without form, and void; and darkness was upon the face of the deep. (Genesis 1v2).**

Many theologians believe that this description of the earth is after the fall of Satan into the earthly realm...because when God creates, He does all things perfectly and in Order. **1 Corinthians 14 v33** says, **"For God is not the author of confusion..."**

**1 John 1v5 ...God is light, and in him there is no darkness at all.**

Satan has corrupted the order of God on the earth and made it a place of dishonour. The moment you take the order of God out of anything, you create dishonour. We can see the effects of this in our societies, schools, homes, governments etc. Please remember this throughout the book as you read.

**God Has an Order ...**
For honouring your parents
For honouring government

For honouring your pastor
For honouring your husband or wife
For honouring your children
For honouring leadership in any environment.

The purpose of the devil is to destroy that order, so that mankind will live in dishonour and lose the blessing of God.

**John 10v10 explains that the devil steals, kills and destroys.**

One day I sat with a man who told me of his first marriage and things that went wrong. He explained to me how his ex-wife chased him down the road with a brick in her hand. I started laughing as he was telling me this and we both had a good laugh.

A few months later the Holy Spirit reminded me of that story and said, *"The earth is so filled with dishonour that you laugh at it when you see or hear it"*, because that is so dishonouring for any human to do to another. Then He said, *"Humans has been so polluted with dishonour that honour looks strange to them, they are offended when they see it."*

We attended a funeral a while back and my son got up to assist his mother when she went onto the platform. As she walked up the stairs, he held her hand for support, the audience started laughing, finding this act of honour very strange. After she paid her tribute he walked up to her again and assisted her down the stairs, this got the people laughing again. These where adults laughing at my sixteen-year-old son, showing his mother honour.

When children show their parents honour, other kids laugh at them because it's "uncool".

When we show our bosses honour at work, our colleagues accuse us of being a back biter.

If we honour our pastors or church leaders, we cannot be part of the clique...... because **Honour** is strange to the atmosphere of the earth.

Always remember that your loyalty should be to the highest authority in any environment. If your colleague at work is trying to influence you and others against your supervisor, your loyalty is to your supervisor. If your supervisor is trying to influence you and others against your CEO, your loyalty is to your CEO. The only authority that overrides the highest level of authority in any environment, is God… He is our highest authority. This does not mean if your earthly authority does not live by God's word that you don't have to obey them.

I remember when I was in my twenties and my boss was an atheist. I never spoke to him at work about God, it would be out of order as I was there to work and not preach. However, there were moments when he gave me a ride home from work and I would use those opportunities to talk to him about the things of God. He appreciated the fact that I wasn't bible bashing people in the hours that he was paying me to work. I was taught by my parents that the only bible many people will read, is the life they see me live. He understood my love for Jesus but was also pleased that I honoured him as my boss. Years later, I started my own company and I still had access to him as an advisor in my business. When you show honour to your authorities, they will honour you with the greatest gift anyone can give you – the gift of access. The prayer that Jesus taught us is so powerful …

Our Father who art in Heaven
Hallowed be thy name
**Thy Kingdom Come,**
**Thy Will Be Done on Earth as It Is in Heaven...**
We need heaven's atmosphere of Glory and Honour on the earth.

Our churches should be an example of heaven on earth, where the gathering of God's people produces glory and honour. I have seen much of the glory of God in our gatherings through the years, but I am sad to say not much honour. I hear statements like "everything you need is in the glory" … if that is true, why do our people stay broke? The glory produces different results than honour.

The glory produces:
- A hunger for God
- It revives your spirit
- It increases the anointing
- It's the birthplace for creative miracles.

Honour produces:

- Favour
- Promotion
- Blessing
- Increase.

Whatever is created in the glory must be honoured (kept in order), to enjoy the rewards of it. The children of Israel wondered with Moses in the desert and saw the manifestation of God's glory many times. However, their murmuring came before God as a proof of their dishonour, not valuing the order of God.

I have minister friends whom I love dearly that have great anointing's and in a moment, can bring down the glory of God in a building ... but they are struggling to produce any fruits of increase in their ministries, because I have also seen their dishonour to others. There is proof of the glory, but no proof of honour, because they violate the order of God in the house of God.

People who grow up in a Godly home where the order of God is being enforced by the parents, often do better in ministry than those who start serving God from adulthood. Order shapes your character into a life of honour, while the glory creates a hunger for God. Many who start late in God's kingdom is hungry for the glory of God, but they lack the honour that the Order of God produces and they don't experience all that God has for them. You need the **MASTER KEY OF HONOUR** to open doors for you, as you journey through life. Dr Murdock believes, if you have not been taught honour by the age of twenty, you will struggle to learn it and live by it.

My friend, do not get swallowed up by the dishonour of this world that the devil has brought about by corrupting God's order.  If your dishonour has cost you dearly, it's not

too late to turn it around, by starting to live
a life of honour.

**The Good News**

 Everything God expects of us to do has
rewards.

 **Luke 6v38; Deut.8; Deut.28**

God is a rewarder - **Hebrews 11v6 … He is
also not a man that He would lie…. Has He
said it shall He not do it? – (Numbers
23v19).**

As human beings we are reward-driven,
everything we do is for a reward. God
knows this that is why He offers us rewards
all the time.

When you give your life to Him for a prayer
of salvation, He offers you eternal life with a
mansion in heaven, if you remain faithful to
the end.

In everyday life, we look for rewards. You
can love your boss and think that he is

wonderful, but the reason you are working for him, is for that salary at the end of the month.

When you give your child anything and they don't say "thank you", you are upset because their thankfulness is your reward.

**Honour Has Rewards**

When you honour your parents, you create favour and they bless you.

When you honour your boss, you create favour and promotion will follow.

When you honour your pastor, you create favour and he will trust you with things he cannot trust others with.

**Wisdom key:** Where there is honour, there is favour and where there is favour, there is blessing and money. Dr Mike Murdock.

# CHAPTER 3

**WHY HONOUR IS SO DIFFICULT FOR US**

**Pride Will Stop You from Honouring Fools Can't Show Honour**

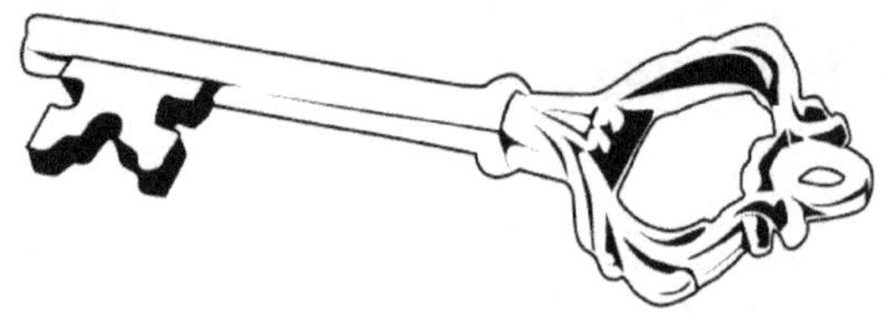

<u>Wisdom key:</u>

A proud person cannot give honour...And a proud person cannot receive honour

- Ps Clint Ross

## 1.  Pride will stop you from honouring.

**A man's pride shall bring him low: but Honour shall uphold the humble in spirit. (Proverbs 29v23)**

The root cause of us not being able to show honour is our pride.

The bible has numerous scriptures that tells us who to honour and how to honour them, but we fight it because we don't want to acknowledge the importance of another person. Our pride is the reason why there are many things that God cannot do through us. Prideful people always think they are better than others and can never see the greatness of achievers.

*Humility is not what you think of yourself… Humility is what you think of others!*

Growing up, I had one of our neighbours always telling me that he was only a worm in the dust and nobody important. That is not humility my friend, you must know that you are the crown of God's creation and that you are very important. When this same man spoke of others, you could hear that he thought of himself better than them. A truly humble person will know his value and acknowledge the value of others.

Let me remind you that **Pride Goeth Before Destruction… (Proverbs 16v18)**

**God dwells with the humble… (Isaiah 57v15)**

**God resists the proud, but gives grace to the humble… (James 4v6)**

That means that when you are humble God plays on your team, but when you are prideful he plays for the opposing team. My friend, you don't want God to resist you. God's team always wins. This book will be a pride detector in your life.

People who are carnal and full of pride find it hard to submit to God's word. They always want to add worldly philosophies to justify their prideful beliefs.

2. **Fools can't show honour.**

**As snow in summer, and rain in harvest, so honour is not seemly for a fool. (Proverbs 26v1)**

This simply means that the day you see snow fall in the middle of summer, a fool will understand honour.

Ignorance is when you don't know.

Foolishness is when you are taught, but you don't want to know. Dr Mike Murdock has a whole chapter on fools in his book **The Law of Recognition.** A must-read to have more understanding of fools.

**Fools despise wisdom and instruction (Proverbs 1v7).**

**The fool said in his heart, there is no God. (Psalm 14v1)**

Honour is hard to learn, but it's even harder to teach. People always fight anyone who tries to teach honour, because they think it is for control. However, as you read further you will discover that honour is to all people, not only those in authority. You deserve the honour due to you.

The devil does not want you to discover the key of honour, because he doesn't want you blessed.

Decide in your heart today, that pride and foolishness will not stop you from reaching the blessing God has for you and your generations, through **this Master key of Honour.**

Wisdom, in the book of Proverbs, is often referred to as a "she", because wisdom gives birth to things.

You will find twins that often appear together in the bible that wisdom gives birth to - **Riches and Honour... Riches and honour are with me... (Proverbs 8v18)**

Where there is honour there is riches. Where there is dishonour, in most cases, you will find poverty. In most wealthy

places, rules of order and honour have been established. Most poor places have no order and is filled with dishonour.
A fool struggles to live in an environment where there is order.

# CHAPTER 4

## THE DIFFERENCE BETWEEN HONOUR AND RESPECT

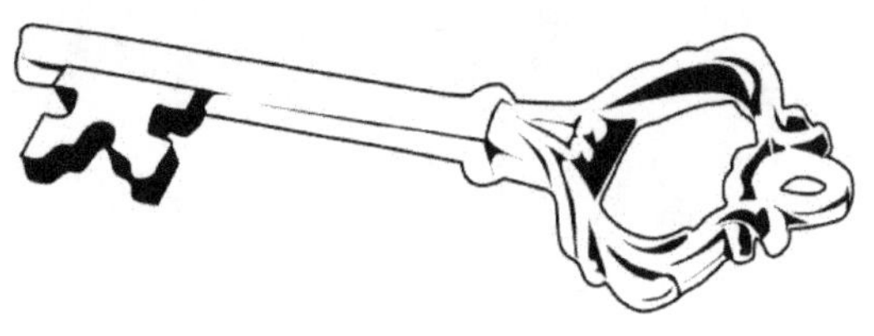

Wisdom key:

If you can only honour God and not the people He used, to get you to where you are... You have pride issues

- Ps Clint Ross

These two are like a hand in a glove, they go together, yet they are different.

Respect is an attitude towards something or someone.

I've heard many people say, "you must earn my respect". If that is so, then it means there is no respect the first time we meet, because I must work to earn it.

I believe respect is a gift and you choose who you want to give it to. This gift, however, can be withdrawn at any time.

When I preach at a church for the first time I often thank the people for their respect. We have just met and they are sitting and listening to me talking for an hour. *That is respect.*

*Honour is when the attitude of respect becomes demonstrated.* It is no longer just a feeling, it becomes an action. So, you can have the attitude of respect and still have pride, but it takes humility to go into action on the instruction of someone else. If after the service, the pastor should ask everyone to pack up the chairs ... those who honour him will go into action, but those who respect him will stand around talking. They are still there, but there is no demonstration.

A man on a bus can respect women, but never demonstrate it by giving them a hand to enter, exit or a seat to sit. *Honour is action.*

Respect to me is like bronze and honour like gold. When you polish them, they can look the same, but they are not. When you neglect to polish bronze it will go dull very quickly, not so with gold. *A heart of gold is a humble heart and shows genuine honour.* With this illustration, I'm not down-playing respect, because it is very important, but I'm merely expressing the value of honour.

Someone who respects you can easily walk away from you, but someone who honours you, have put their energy into the relationship.

# CHAPTER 5

**THE DIFFERENCE BETWEEN WORSHIP AND HONOUR**

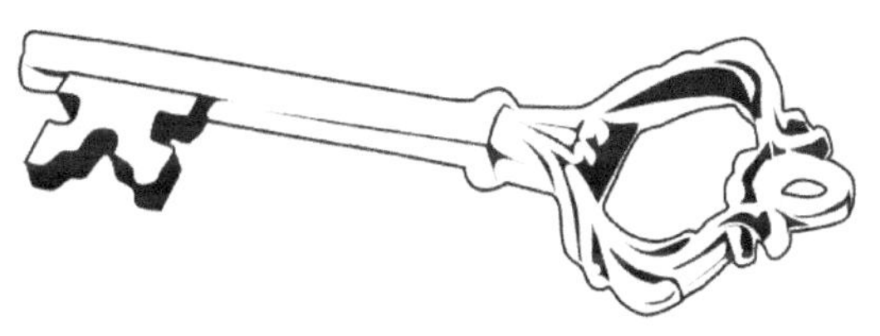

<u>Wisdom key:</u>

Only a fool will worship a man...

And only a fool will show no

honour to a man

- Ps Clint Ross

On numerous occasions I have seen leaders being served and others would say, "I don't worship a man".

I prayed and ask the Holy Spirit to please help me with this, as I don't want to worship a man, neither do I want to fall short in my honour to man.

One day during my time of prayer, about 2 o'clock the afternoon, the following scripture came to mind … **"But the hour cometh and now is, when the true worshippers shall worship the Father in Spirit and in truth … (John 4v23).**

The Holy Spirit started to minister to me that we are body, soul and spirit. One body, with a soul and spirit inside. The spirit is the part that God wants worship to flow from. The soul is your intellect, your mind, the real you, where your pride or humility is.

So, if you kneel before a man to clean his shoes as an act of honour, people are offended, because it's the same posture we use to pray. The problem we have is that we only have one body to demonstrate worship or honour. Honour comes from the soul of man, whereas worship comes from the spirit of man, but we only have one body to demonstrate both.

In the book of **2 Kings chapter 4** is a remarkable story about a Shunammite woman who honoured Elisha by serving him. She is the only woman the bible refers to as great. Her honour to the man of God brought her, her heart's desire, a son. One day, her son died and she went to Elisha to ask for help.

**And when she came to the man of God to the hill, she caught him by the feet: but Gehazi came near to thrust her away. And the man of God said, let her alone; for her Soul is vexed within her. (2 Kings 4v27).**

Her bowing at his feet was not to worship him, but to show honour that comes from her soul. The man of God was wise enough to see and discern this. His servant Gehazi could not.I have seen many times where people want to show a leader honour and then his own assistants get offended. It reminds me of when the woman poured out the oil on Jesus, and Judas became offended. If you are an assistant to someone be careful of familiarity, it can cause you to lose your blessing just like Gehazi and Judas did.

# CHAPTER 6

**THE THREE LEVELS OF HONOUR**

Authority – those above you
Your Peers – those on your level
Your Subordinates – those under your authority

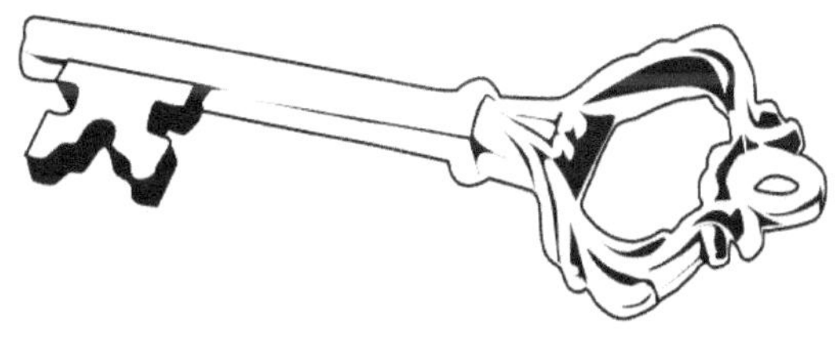

Wisdom key:

Honour is the master key to the blessings

of God.

It unlocks every door in every

environment –Ps Clint Ross

**"Honour all men. Love the brotherhood. Fear God. Honour the King." (1 Peter 2v17)**

**Honour is on three levels**

- Authority - those above you
- Your Peers - those on your level
- Your subordinates - those under you authority.

Each level has different rules and produce different rewards. This chapter is to show you the three levels which will be explained in more detail in the follow chapters.

**Authority**

**Romans 13v1-2 let everyone be subject to the governing authorities, for there is no authority except that which God has established. The authorities that exist have been established by God. Consequently, whoever rebels against the authority is rebelling against what God has instituted, and those who do so will bring judgement on themselves. (NIV)**

*You will always have an authority above you, no matter how high you climb the ladder of life.*

Our first authority is God, then our parents, governmental authorities, our spiritual leaders, our school teachers, our bosses etc.

We should not honour those above us the way *we think* they should be honoured, we should honour them the way They *Want* to be honoured. It is important for you to find out how your authorities want to be honoured. This will remove frustration from the relationship, because you might have in your mind ways you want to show honour, but those ways might not be how they want to be honoured, leaving both parties frustrated. Those whom you have access to, you must ask.

You will discover that a few of them have not thought this through, so you must be patient in your request. You are also an authority to someone, and if they had to ask you now to name ten things that makes you feel honoured, you would have to

pause and think and maybe get back to
them.

Not everyone has the same things that
make them feel honoured. Although there
are standard things that makes anyone feel
honoured, for example the way we respond
to them and the way we question them etc.
Always ask your authority questions to
extract information and never to challenge
them.

Then there are specific things that could
annoy them, for instance when you answer
your phone while they're talking to you, or
when you get up from the table without
asking to be excused. This might not offend
every authority, but you must make sure,
because you don't want to lose their favour,
which leads you to the blessing. The right
questions will get you the answers that you
need. Never assume, the price of
assumption could be costly.
The bible encourages us to not think of
ourselves more highly than we ought to
**(Romans 12v3).** It is however your
authority's responsibility to remain humble,

and not yours to try and keep them humble. Your responsibility before God is just to show honour to your authorities.

*The rewards of honouring authority are continued access, favour and blessing.*

**Your Peers – Those on Your Level.**

*Your peers deserve your honour.*

**Be not deceived; God is not mocked: for whatsoever a man soweth, that shall he also reap. (Galatians 6v7)**

This scripture should be remembered throughout the entire book, but for this passage I want to put extra emphasis on it, because I know how difficult this one could be.

I have discovered that our peers are the ones we are mostly in competition with and it is hard to show honour when you're in competition, for example in sport, at your job, in ministry, etc.

Competition is good, but its purpose is to bring out the best in us, and not to destroy one another. I have watched the coach of Liverpool football club, Jurgen Klopp and the coach of Huddersfield football club, David Wagner, as their teams play to win against one another, but off the pitch these two coaches are best of friends. They have learnt to appreciate one another's different style of coaching, without becoming bitter when either team wins.

*In the Kingdom of God we are not in competition, but we're into completion. Dr Basil Tryon.*

*Honouring your peers is celebrating the difference in them.* Our similarities are what makes us agree, but our differences are what makes us unique.
In church ministry as an example, we all received different gifts and anointings from God. One man does not contain everything, that's why the bible compares us with the human body consisting of different **parts (1 Corinthians 12v12)**. The eye cannot say it's

more important than the ear, every part is needed for the body to function well.

Is your anointing and gifting important? Without a shadow of doubt, but so is your fellow brother and sister's.

 It is important for you to value and celebrate your gift and anointing, and stay focused on God using you in that function.

However, when you honour the gift and anointing on someone else's life, the grace of that person's gift and anointing will start to increase in your life.

I believe when you honour the difference in your peers, God is honoured because He has created them with that difference for a reason.

*As You Sow You Will Reap....*
The rewards of honouring your peers are... the way you celebrate others, is the way you will be celebrated.

**Your Subordinates – Those Under Your Authority.**

**Foolishness is bound in the heart of a child; but the rod of correction shall drive him far from it. (Proverbs 22v15)**

 You may think that this is a strange scripture to use for honour, but that is an honour-scripture.

I will write in the context of parenting, but it applies to pastors, bosses or any authoritative figure....the parents to their children, the pastor to his congregation and the boss to his employees.

Correction to your subordinates is the way you honour them.

If a parent never corrects a child, he has destroyed the future of that child. The way a child responds to a parent, will tell you the future of a child. *Parents are the first authority that God gives us on the earth.* The way we respond to them, is the way we will respond to every other authority afterwards.

Any correction upward is a sign of rebellion, but correction downward, is a proof of your honour.

When you want to honour the authority above you, a monetary gift is one of the first things you can do. When you honour your subordinates, you give them correction, encouragement, advice, etc but money is one of the last things.

Money is based on a reward system. Your boss doesn't pay you because you are cute, he pays you because you've solved a problem for him. You've first worked, and then the reward of money came, in the form of your salary. You give your boss the best of your energy, mind, relationship etc. and your reward is money. So your money represents the best of you, which is why it is such a valuable gift to give your authority, as proof of your honour. Even God wants money first and feels honoured by it.

I believe, if you give your kids money every time they ask for it, without teaching them to earn it as a reward, you have destroyed their future. When a parent however needs money, it should be an honour for a child to give it. The people who have paid things for you for most of your young life, deserves your gift of monetary honour.

You must correct those under your authority when they go wrong. It is proof that you are interested in their future and that is proof of your honour to them. Also, teach them how you want to be honoured, so that you don't live frustrated as explained earlier.

The rewards of honouring your subordinates... you show how much you care by developing them for their future. Your life is also free from frustration, as they know what is expected of them.

# CHAPTER 7

**HOW GOD WANTS TO BE HONOURED**

**God feels Honoured when He is Trusted**
**God feels Honoured when His Instructions are followed Correctly**
**God feels Honoured when you are Zealous about what He is Zealous About**
**God is Honoured through the Full Tithe and Proper Offerings**

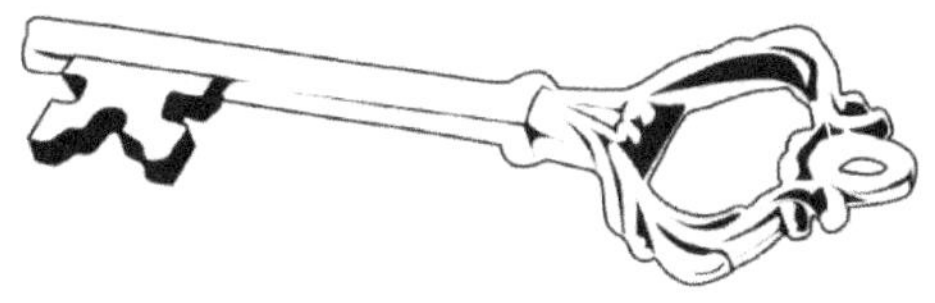

Wisdom key:

Your dishonour has cost you dearly...

But you can turn it around and live in the

blessing that honour brings

- Ps Clint Ross

**Wherefore the Lord said, Forasmuch as this people draw near me with their mouth, and with their lips do honour me, but have removed their heart far from me, and their feet towards me is taught by the precept of men. (Isaiah 29v13)**

As previously mentioned in the book, that you should not honour someone the way you think they should be honoured, you should honour them the way they want to be honoured.

God is very specific in the bible on how He wants to be honoured.

1. **God feels honoured when He is trusted.**

**Numbers 20v6-12 (NIV) Moses and Aaron went from the assembly to the entrance to the tent of Meeting and fell facedown, and the glory of the Lord appeared to them. The Lord said to Moses, "Take the staff, and you and your brother Aaron gather the assembly together. Speak to that rock before their eyes and it will pour out its water. You will bring water out of the rock**

**for the community so that their livestock can drink." So Moses took the staff from the Lord's presence, just as He commanded him. He and Aaron gathered the assembly together in front of the rock and Moses said to them, "Listen, you rebels, must we bring you water out of this rock?" Then Moses raised his arm and struck the rock twice with his staff. Water gushed out, and the community and their livestock drank, but the Lord said to Moses and Aaron, "Because you did not Trust me enough to Honour Me as holy in the sight of the Israelites, you will not bring this community into the land I give them."**

Doubt is something the devil has brought into the atmosphere of the earth, corrupting it with dishonour, which brings pain to the heart of God. He caused Adam and Eve to doubt the words of God and lose the blessing God had for them.

In the book of **Numbers chapter 13**, Moses sent twelve leaders to explore the land of Canaan and spy it for forty days. Ten leaders came back with a doubt report and

the other two with a faith report. Moses believed the ten and caused the Israelites to spend forty years in the desert. Forty days to spy the land, forty years of pain because he believed a doubt report...*Doubt is deadlier than we think.*
The devil knows that your faith in God pleases God, so if he can cause you to doubt God, he has not only caused you to lose your blessing, but it will also bring pain to the heart of God.

**Wisdom key:** God's greatest pain is to be doubted... God's greatest joy is to be believed. Dr Mike Murdock.

When we trust God completely, He feels honoured. Don't allow doubt to rob you of all the blessings that God has for you. Make God proud by displaying faith in Him at all times, it brings pleasure to His heart and makes Him feel honoured.

**Hebrews 11v6 says, "But without faith it is impossible to please Him, for he that cometh to God must believe that He is, and**

**that He is a rewarder of them that diligently seek Him.”**

2.  **God feels honoured when his instructions are followed correctly.**

 In the book of **Numbers 20v6-12** we read that God gave Moses specific instructions to speak to the rock, instead he struck it twice. Moses never entered the promised land because he never followed God's instruction properly. Receiving instructions from God is not always easy to follow through. As you grow in faith, it seems like God's instructions gets more difficult, but I have consoled myself with knowing that the difficult instructions mean that God can trust me more. His instructions many times seem illogical, but remember, that is what faith is about. If it all made sense when He gave us the instruction, it would require no faith. Therefore, the peace we have, is that God will always reward us for our obedience.

**Isaiah 1v19 - If you are willing and obedient, you will eat the good things of the land.**

*One of The Hardest Instructions I Had to Follow.*

I remember many years ago, God gave me an instruction to bless someone with my Mercedes Benz. I have always wanted to obey God in my giving. Knowing that He will bless me, as I have been taught by various mentors from God's word, especially Dr Murdock, who has an amazing understanding about this. This car was my dream car. I was young and very proud to be able to drive a car like this. I barely had the car for a year and was still really enjoying it.

One day, I attended a conference and the Holy Spirit instructed me to bless the man that was preaching, with my car. I first tried to ignore His whispers, but it grew stronger and stronger, till I could no longer focus on what the preacher was saying. I remember leaning over to my wife and telling her what

I heard the Holy Spirit was telling me, hoping she would speak some sense into me and stop me.  Her response was in a whisper to me, *"If God is speaking to you then you better obey."* This was my only car, I was still paying the bank. I didn't have the money to buy another car, all these thoughts went through my mind. Then some of the wisdom keys of Dr Murdock came to mind.

- The seed that leaves your hand never leaves your life but enters into your future where it multiplies.
- Nothing leaves heaven until something leaves the earth.
- When God speaks to you about a seed, He already has a harvest on His mind.

The Holy Spirit ministered to me*," Never give out of calculation, give out of revelation.*

Then worry turned into excitement, I jumped up and said to the preacher, "I want to bless you with my car!" That whole meeting erupted with the spirit of generosity. People started giving and blessing one another.

This was at a time when I had a new company and was really believing God for work in the business. Two months later, I was blessed with a contract ten times the value that the car I sowed was. The work, for my new company I was believing God for, came after obeying an instruction from God.

*The Rewards of Trusting God and Following His Instruction: You will enter your promised land.*

3. **God feels honoured when you are zealous about what He is zealous about.**

**Phinehas son of Eleazar, the son of Aaron, the priest, has turned my anger away from the Israelites; for he was as zealous as I am for my honour among them... (Numbers 25v11) (NIV).**

He and his descendants will have a covenant of a lasting priesthood, because he was zealous for my honour... (Numbers 25v13) (NIV)

Zeal and passion are two great forces, which can cause us to accomplish many things in this world. There are things that God also has zeal for.

*God is zealous about justice, peace, judgement and what He has established.*

John 2v16 And said unto them that sold doves, take these things hence; make not my Father's house an house of merchandise, and his disciples remembered that it was written, The Zeal of Thine House Hath Eaten Me Up.

Isaiah 9v7 - Of the increase of his government and peace there shall be no end, upon the throne of David, upon his kingdom, to order it, and to establish it with Judgement and with justice from henceforth even for ever. The Zeal of the Lord of hosts will perform this.

In **Numbers chapter 25** the men of Israel began to indulge in sexual immorality with Moabite women and started to worship the Baal of Peor. One Israelite went before the eyes of Moses and the assembly into a tent, with a Midianite woman. Phinehas was so upset that he entered the tent, took a spear and drove it through both of them. God was pleased with this and stopped the plague over them.

It is important for us as God's children, that His zeal consumes us. This world we are living in has lost the fear of God and with that has dishonoured Him.

*The Reward of Being Zealous for God and The Things of God:* God will establish a covenant for your descendants.

God said about Phinehas, **"He and his descendants will have a covenant of a lasting priesthood, because he was zealous for my honour..." (Numbers 25v13) (NIV)**

## 4. God is honoured through the full tithe and proper offerings.

The most famous scripture about honouring God that most of us know is **Proverbs 3v9. Honour the Lord with thy substance, and with the first fruits of all thine increase.**

God is explaining to us what makes Him feel honoured, and then tells us the reward in **verse 10 ... So shall thy barns be filled with plenty, and thy presses shall burst out with new wine.**

I will explain this further from the book of Malachi. In the book of Malachi, God is explaining to the nation of Israel, how He wants to be honoured. The book starts with these words, "The burden of the word of the Lord to Israel". God is burdened with something.

**In verse 6 of chapter 1** God asked them this question," **A son honoureth his father and a servant his master: if then I be a father, where is mine honour? ... O priests, that**

**despise my name? And you say, wherein have we despised thy name?**

God feels dishonoured by them and here is the reason. **Verse 7** He says," **Ye offer polluted bread upon mine altar**..." In **verse 8** He says," **And if ye offer the blind for sacrifice, is it not evil? And if ye offer the lame and sick, is it not evil? Offer it now unto thy governor; will he be pleased with thee**..."

God is not offended because they are bringing offerings. It is the kind of offerings that they are bringing that He is not happy with. They are not bringing their best, and this makes Him feel dishonoured. In **verse 10** He says," **I have no pleasure in you... neither will I accept an offering at your hand.**"

I train our people at church, when they bring their offerings to God, they must always make it is presentable. No matter the amount, if you believe it is the best you are giving, don't fold it in a closed hand.

Open it up, make it presentable to God and be proud of your offering.

Does God feel honoured when he sees your offerings?

In **Chapter 2v1-3** God says," **And now, O ye priests, this commandment is for you. If you will not hear, and if ye will not lay it to heart, to give glory unto my name, saith the Lord of host, I will even send a curse upon you, and I will curse your blessings: yea, I have cursed them already, because you do not lay it to heart. Behold I will corrupt your seed, and spread dung up on your faces."**

Man! That sounds like someone who is not just offended, but mad at them. God expected the priests to make sure that the offerings the people are bringing Him, are proper offerings that will make Him feel honoured. Even today, when a pastor speaks about offerings the people get upset, but it's his responsibility before God, to make sure they give proper offerings in honour to Him.

**Chapter 3v3 And he shall sit as a refiner and purifier of silver: and he shall purify the sons of Levi, and purge them as gold and silver, that they may offer unto the Lord an offering in righteousness.**

*God is honoured through proper offerings.*

The final question God asked them in **Chapter 3v8.**

**Will a man rob God?**

**They reply by asking, wherein have we robbed thee?**

**And He answers, In Tithes and Offerings...**

God explains to them the rewards that will come to them, if they will just honour Him.

**Bring ye all the tithes into the storehouse, that there may be meat in my house, and prove me now herewith, saith the Lord of hosts, if I will not open you the windows of heaven, and pour you out a blessing, that**

**there shall not be room enough to receive it. (Malachi 3v10)**

What a great promise from God to us. In this verse, you will find it is the only time God says that He will prove to you His existence. The Holy Spirit said to me once," you will be my window on the earth that I pour my blessings through." My dear friend, God is honoured through our tithes and offerings. God ends the book of Malachi with this scripture... **And he shall turn the heart of the fathers to the children, and the heart of the children to their fathers, lest I come and smite the earth with a curse. (Malachi 4v6).**

After that God goes quiet for 400 years, until He brings His son Jesus into the earth, to teach us how the Father should be honoured. *The Rewards of Honouring God with The Full Tithe and Proper Offerings*: He opens up the windows of heaven over your life and removes the curse.

# CHAPTER 8

**HONOURING YOUR PASTOR**

**What is Double Honour**
**Your Pastor is a Gift from God**

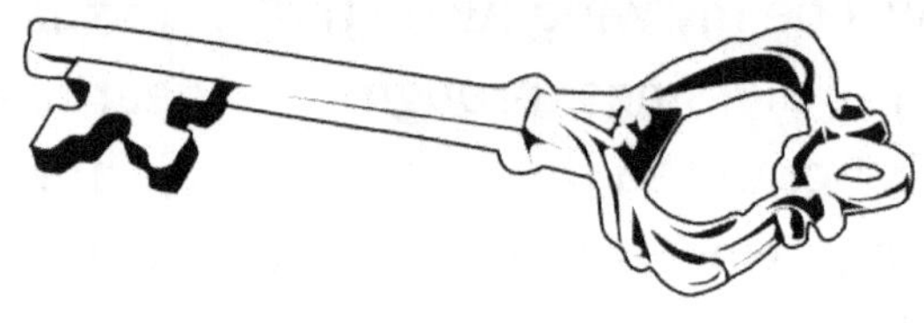

Wisdom key:

Honouring a man of God is one of the greatest ways the anointing of that man will come upon your life

-Ps Clint Ross

*The word pastor simply means shepherd,*
but it is someone who watches over people.
Jesus said He is the good shepherd,
meaning He is the good pastor. Many
people call their spiritual leaders different
names, but whatever that name may be, if
they are the ones watching over your
spiritual well-being, then I am referring to
them in this chapter.

Let the elders (pastors) that rule well, be
counted worthy of **Double Honour,**
especially they who labour in the word and
doctrine. For the scripture saith, **thou shalt
not muzzle the ox that treadeth out the
corn. And, the labourer is worthy of his
wage. (1Timothy 5v17-18)**

Your pastor is the only one who God says, is
worthy of double honour. God does not
even say that about Himself. God must then
have a very high opinion of a pastor.
Therefore, if God does, then I would
encourage you to do the same. Think about
this for a moment, God himself comes to
earth in the form of a man, His son Jesus.
He could choose any job on the planet, but

He chose to be a good pastor. He didn't become the CEO of a fishing or carpentry company, He chose the work of the ministry. That leads me to believe that in the mind of God, it is the most important job on the planet.

**What is double honour?**

I've read different opinions about this, but I will pass on to you, what I have received from the Holy Spirit.

Jesus said in **John 12v26, "If any man serve me, let him follow me; and where I am, there shall also my servant be: if any man serve me, him will my Father honour.**

The pastor is often referred to as the servant of the Lord. I know many people say they are the servants of the Lord, but they are not in the capacity of the pastor, who has abandoned all to follow and serve full time in the work of the Lord.

So that scripture explains to us, that God the Father honours a pastor. He honours the pastor so much, that the tithe He asks for as proof for honouring Him, He says it belongs to the pastor.  In **Numbers 18v21** God says, **"I have given the children of Levi (pastors) all the tenth in Israel for an inheritance, for their service which they serve, even the service of the tabernacle of the congregation.**

**Hebrews 7v5 - And verily they that are of the sons of Levi, who receive the office of priesthood, have a commandment to take tithes of the people...**

If you give your tithe to God and He gives it to the pastor, you've given your pastor nothing yet. God gives His portion, to the pastor. I call that vertical honour. Your portion that you give to your pastor, is horizontal honour. Remember, honour is action.

**Obey them that have the rule over you, and submit yourselves: for they watch for your souls, as they that must give account, that they may do it with joy, and not with**

**grief: for that is unprofitable for you. (Hebrews 13v17)**

*You honour your pastor by:*
- Listening to him
- Following his instructions
- Sowing generously to him.

Dr Murdock teaches us that we are a walking warehouse of seeds.

- Love is a seed
- Kindness is seed
- Forgiveness is a seed
- Money is a seed
- Patience is a seed, etc.

Start sowing seeds into your pastor today, it is proof of your honour.

*God gets vertical honour from you ... heavenly level.*

*Your pastor gets horizontal honour from you ... earthly level.*

*All other authorities in your life get horizontal honour... earthly level*

So, God honouring your pastor is vertical honour (heavenly level) and you honouring your pastor is horizontal honour (earthly level) hence, your pastor gets both vertical and horizontal honour.

That is how I see Double Honour.

The gospel of **Luke 2v52** says that **Jesus (the good pastor) increased in wisdom and stature, and in favour with God and Man.**

**What I Have Learned from Pastor Ana Sweet That Has Changed My Life**

We were at a conference in Kenya, where Dr Murdock was the keynote speaker. At lunch Pastor Ana and I sat with a few other people at the same table. She started sharing her testimony of loyalty towards her pastor as a young girl. She then made this statement, the most important person in your life is the one who builds your faith. Explaining from the scriptures in **1 John 5v4**

**that faith is the victory that overcomes the world.** Whoever then is building your faith, is causing you to live a life of overcoming and victory. She was quoting **Hebrews 11v6, without faith it is impossible to please God...** The one building your faith is the one keeping you pleasing God. When God is pleased with you, His blessing will be seen in your life.

This does not mean that hard times will not come, but the faith that your pastor is building in you, will cause you to overcome and live the blessed life.

After she explained her testimony of loyalty to her pastor and the rewards it brought, she turned to me and asked, *"What will make you leave your pastor?"*

- When he goes through a tough time?
- When other people leave, will you leave?
- When accusations come against him?

Your answer will tell you what your level of commitment, loyalty and honour is towards

him ... remembering that this is the same man who stood with you through your difficult times.
If God's honour is so generous towards your pastor, make sure you do the same in your honour to him.

**Your pastor is a gift from God.**

**And I will give you pastors according to mine heart, which shall feed you with knowledge and understanding. And it shall come to pass, when ye be multiplied and increased in the land... (Jeremiah 3v15-16).**

God will send a man of God into your life to pastor you. You don't choose your pastor, you discover him. His teachings will bring you to an understanding of God and your assignment upon the earth. This will cause you to multiply and increase.

The way you receive a gift sends a message to the giver of the gift of your appreciation or ungratefulness.  The way you treat your pastor (God's gift to you), sends God a message of whether He knows what you need or not. If you believe that God knows what is best for your life, then you should value the gift He sent you.

The bible refers to men as trees.

A Revelation I received…

There are a few times in the bible where people are referred to as trees.

**Psalm 1v3. And he shall be like a Tree planted by the by the rivers of water, that bringeth forth his fruit in his season.**

**Psalm 52v8 But I am like a green olive TREE in the house of God…**

**Mark 8v24 - And he looked up, and said, I see men as trees, walking.**

Now switch on your imagination with me for a moment … the colour of the leaves of a tree is green, so is the colour of the dollar which is the world currency.

**Revelation 22v2 …. And the leaves of the TREE were for the healing of the nations.**

Money is an important tool that is used to bring healing to nations. The purpose of money is to create ability, to fulfil a dream or vision. In the kingdom of God, God gives His servants (pastors) vision to bring healing to this world. The money to fulfil that vision, is with the people God assigns to him.

**Mark 11v13. And seeing a fig tree afar off having leaves, he came, if haply he might find anything thereon: and when he came to it, he found nothing but leaves.**

We know that Jesus was so disappointed when He only found leaves and no fruit on the tree, that He cursed the tree. It was the leaves that drew Him, but it's the fruits that would have blessed Him. Money alone is not good enough, you need a purpose and vision for your money, to bring healing to this lost and dying world. It is not good enough that your tree has leaves on it, but it needs fruit otherwise you will be cursed. **(Malachi 3v9).**

**Luke 13v6-9 He spake also this parable; A certain man had a fig tree planted in his vineyard; and he came and sought fruit theron, and found none. Then said he unto the dresser of his vineyard, Behold, these three years I come seeking fruit on this tree, and find none: cut it down; why cumbereth it the ground? And he answering said unto him, Lord, let it alone this year also, till I shall dig about it, and dung it: And if it bear fruit, well: and if not, then after that thou shalt cut it down.**

For the purpose of what I am trying to explain, God is the certain man, your pastor is the dresser of His vineyard and you are the fig tree.

In this story, there are also only leaves on the tree and no fruit. God is not impressed with leaves only, He wants to see fruit too. Your pastor, as the dresser, is the one who has to work with you to produce those fruits. He however, can only help you as far as you will allow him to.

We read in **Jeremiah 3v15** that God gives pastors to teach knowledge and understanding. It is his job to help you gain knowledge from God and bring you to a place of understanding, between knowledge and understanding is wisdom. The pastor gives you knowledge, but when you apply it, it becomes wisdom. When your wisdom has produced and you see the results of it, you now have understanding. The dresser (pastor) said, give me a year to dig it. You getting knowledge, is your pastors job, but the application thereof (wisdom) is yours. Whatever your pastor teaches you, the choice to apply it or not, is yours. That is why the dresser said, "Give me a year." Therefore, it was the trees decision, to receive the treatment and produce fruit.

**Proverbs 4v7** says, **Wisdom is the principle thing.** The knowledge you're gaining means nothing, if you are not applying it and don't come to a place of understanding. When you have understanding, no one can argue with you about your beliefs, because you have seen the results of your wisdom. If you are offended every time he speaks to you about the vision God gave him and your financial contribution, you will bear no fruit and a time will come, when God will cut you off as in the story above.

**Matthew 12v33. Either make a tree good, and his fruit good; or else make a tree corrupt, and his fruit corrupt: For A Tree Is Known by His Fruit.**

In God's kingdom, the primary function of the pastor, is to hear from God and share the vision he receives. The primary function of the people with him, is to grow in God's grace as they are taught and bring provision for the vision. The people whose lives are being touched and changed by the gospel of Jesus Christ, through your support, are the fruits on your tree. God wants to see fruit on your tree and not just leaves.

**Note to the Pastor.**

*Even though God sends us people to help fund the vision He gave us, we must never make them our source, as He alone wants to be depended on for our provision.*

**Galatians 3v13 …. Cursed is everyone that hangeth on a tree.**

# CHAPTER 9

## HONOURING YOUR PARENTS

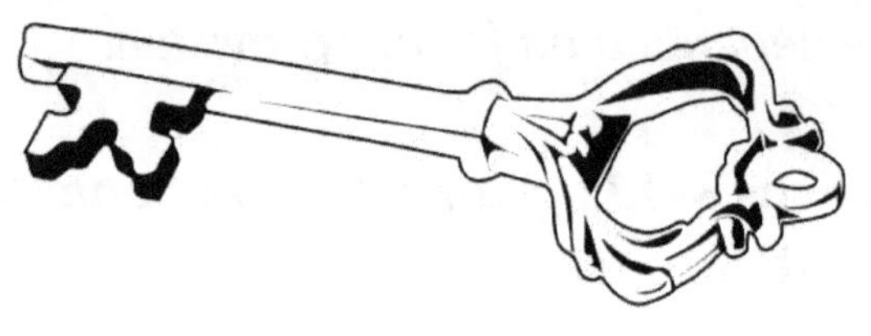

Wisdom key:

When your authority offends you...

Your honour will be tested

- Ps Clint Ross

**Honour thy father and thy mother: that thy days may be long upon the land which the Lord thy God giveth thee. (Exodus 20v12)**

This is one of the ten commandments God gave Moses, but it is the only one with a promise.

Your parents are the first authority God gives you upon the earth. I believe this scripture tells us that the way we respond to our parents, is the way we will respond to every other authority after them and that determines how blessed we will be upon the earth. If you are rude to your parents as a child, you will be rude to your teachers, a police officer and even your boss in the workplace.

*This will cause you to lose favour with authority.*

- When you need that extra marks to make your next grade your teacher will decline it.

- The police officer that could have just let you go with a warning, will find a way to make things difficult for you.
- Your boss will look for every opportunity to get rid of you.

*Honouring your parents affects your whole destiny.*

*God is so big on a father, He calls himself Father.* Throughout the scriptures there are examples of fathers being able to bless or curse you.

*The story of Noah*

Noah had 3 sons Shem, Ham and Japheth. One day after the flood, Noah planted a vineyard. He made wine and drank a little too much of it. As he laid naked and drunk in his tent, his one son Ham saw him and went and told his brothers. Shem and Japheth went in and covered their father's nakedness. When Noah woke up and heard what Ham did, he cursed his generations to be slaves to his brothers.  This story is found in **Genesis chapter 9.**

Ham dishonoured his father and was cursed...

Shem and Japheth honoured their father and were blessed...

*The story of Ruth*

Another story is that of Ruth. God was so impressed with this woman, that He names a book in the bible after her.

We don't know much about her family and upbringing, but the way she treats her mother-in-law says much about the honour she had been taught. Ruth and another woman Orpah, was married to Naomi's sons. After the death of both her sons, Naomi had no expectations of her daughters-in-law to stay with her. Orpah returned home, but Ruth took her as a mother and gave her the honour that a daughter would. Listen to her words in **Ruth 1v16-17. "And Ruth said, intreat me not to leave thee, or to return from following after thee: for whither thou goest, I will go; and where thou lodgest, I will lodge: thy**

**people shall be my people, and thy God my God. Where thou diest, will I die, and there will I be buried: the Lord do so to me, and more also, if ought but death part thee and me.**

Wow, what great loyalty, respect and honour in those words. When you read the story, you will see it was not only words, but it turned into action.

Ruth later met a great, wealthy and influential man named Boaz. Ruth receives favour from him, because he heard how she had honoured her mother-in-law. When he blessed her, she fell on her face to the ground in front of him in thankfulness. Her honour blessed him so much that he finally marries her and the blessed life God promises for honouring, came to pass for Ruth.

Bear in mind that Naomi is not her biological mother but takes the place and role of a mother in her life. God will send people into your life that will take the role of a father or mother in your life and they deserve your honour too. It could be an uncle, aunt, grandmother, grandfather, neighbour, step-father or step-mother.

**1 Corinthians 4v15 says," For though ye have ten thousand instructors in Christ, yet have ye not Many Fathers... "Not many" speaks of more than one.**

Always seek the blessing of your father and mother that it might go well with you … whoever they may be that God has appointed to play that role in your life.

*Choose today to live a life of honour toward any father or mother God places in your life.*

# CHAPTER 10

## HONOUR IN THE MARRIAGE

**Why a Woman Struggles to Show
Honour to Her Husband
How a Man Dishonours His Wife
Why a Man Needs a Pastor**

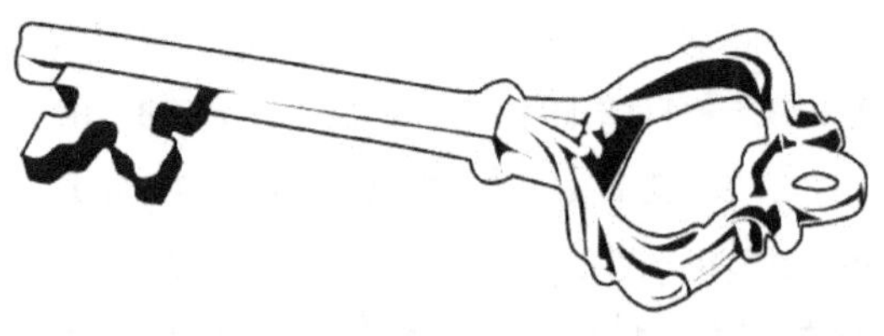

Wisdom key:

Honour is demonstrated in a

woman's submission to her husband...

And honour is demonstrated in a

man's love for his wife - Ps Clint Ross

Marriage is honourable in all, and the bed
undefiled... (Hebrews 13v4)

The highest level of honour a couple can show one another, is to be faithful to the vows they made on their wedding day.

Many people have said that the number one cause of divorce is financial pressure. I believe it is a lack of honour. You can lose all your finances, but still make it through if the honour between the two of you stays intact.

The church and marriage are the two institutions God has established on earth. It is also the two things the devil fights the most. As you read this chapter, remember that you have an enemy that hates your marriage.

**Wives, submit yourselves unto your own husbands, as unto the Lord. For the husband is the head of the wife, even as Christ is the head of the church...
(Ephesians 5v22-23)**

**Likewise, ye husbands, dwell with them according to knowledge, giving honour unto the wife, as unto the weaker vessel,**

**and as being heirs together of the grace of life; that your prayers be not hindered. (1 Peter 3v7)**

There are many different trains of thought around this, but I will do my best to explain what I believe, honour in the marriage should be.

The wife should see her husband as an authority, not as a peer in her life, submitting to his leadership and guidance. The way she responds and speak to him, should be as to an authority.

The husband should however, see her as a peer and honour her as such. Valuing her difference as is explained in a previous chapter about honouring our peers. To him, she should not be seen as a subordinate, because that will put her on the level of his children, which he does not want her to be, but a companion and help meet.

**Why A Woman Struggles to Show Honour**

**1.  She is fighting in the wrong realm**

In **Genesis chapter 3** after Adam and Eve sinned, God speaks 3 curses. One over the serpent (the devil), one over the woman and one over the man.

**Genesis 3v15 God says to the serpent," I will put enmity between thee and the woman...**

This is part of the curse that was spoken over the devil, where he will fight with the woman. Notice this fight, does not include the man. The woman has been designed by God to have supernatural endurance and persistence. What God was telling the devil is, you will fight someone who does not give up easily. That is why you will find women are of the best prayer warriors and intercessors. This endurance and persistence in battle, is however many times used on the wrong opponent, her husband, instead of the devil. She's fighting in the wrong realm.  Many women can argue about the same thing for three days and not be tired. A man argues for one hour, gets in his car and leaves.

### 2.  She is cursed with conflict.

God then speaks a curse over the woman in **Genesis 3v16, Unto the woman he said, I will greatly multiply thy sorrow and thy conception; in sorrow, thou shall bring forth children; and thy desire shall be to thy husband and he shall rule over thee.**

That last part does not sound like a curse, but to fully understand it, you must read **chapter 4v7** where God speaks to Cain in the same way, saying, **"... sin lieth at the door, and unto thee shall be his desire, and thou shalt rule over him.**

God was telling Cain that sin wants to control him, but he must rule over it.

The woman has been made to be the perfect assistant or help meet to her husband. Within her, God built all the attributes of submission and loyalty to the man.

The curse God speaks over her is that she would want to control her husband, but he will rule over her. This desire for control many times overrides any desire to submit to him and this causes her to be cursed with conflict. Thus, knowing submission is right, but wanting to have control in the marriage. That is why Paul in his letters to the church reminds the woman she must submit to her own husband. I think Paul wrote "own husband" because that same woman will submit to her boss and to her pastor much easier than to her own husband. When you marry her, you cannot believe it is the same woman you dated. The curse is in the marriage. If she dishonours you while you are still dating, don't think that it will get better in the marriage.

*That desire for control can be displayed in many ways:*

- If she wants something and he says no, she deprives him of sex. (A man doesn't want sex, he needs it to function well, like a car needs oil.)

- Her tears can be a form of control. (A woman's tears affect a man.)

- Her silence can be a form of control (The silent treatment.)

- Her temper can be a form of control (screaming and shouting). The man is so scared when she does this, that he easily gives her way, as he might just be blamed of abusing her.

When a man loves a woman like the song says, "he will spend his last dime... sleep out in the rain..."

I believe the devil cannot get his way with a man like a woman can. I'm sure that's why he approached Eve in the garden and not Adam. He knew that Adam would do anything for her.

The man who is the authority in the marriage, finds himself being challenged many times by the one who should assist him. This makes him feel dishonoured. Depending on his personality and character, he might endure it for a while, but it will eventually destroy him.

*Women, within every man lives a king and a fool, the one you speak to, is the one that will respond to you. When you speak to the king in your man, the queen in you will be celebrated. Speak to the fool in him and your house will never become your palace.*

The man has been designed to receive honour, so it is very attractive to him when he sees it or receives it. When he is at work and he receives honour from the women there and not at home, he can easily fall into the trap of temptation. At home, he asks for a cup of the tea and his wife responds, "What is wrong with your hands?" At work, he asks for a cup of tea and the response is, "One or two sugars sir?"

*A woman's looks will catch the eye of a man, but it is her words that will catch his heart.*

I'm fully aware that there are other factors to consider, which affect the behaviour of people, but I'm explaining one of the root causes of dishonour from a woman to a man. (The curse of conflict.)

Me sharing this revelation, is to help a man to dwell with his wife with understanding and help her to overcome this challenge (the curse).

**How a man dishonours his wife.**

Men have a responsibility before God, to lead their wives into the future he has promised her. Men want to be honoured as the authority, but many times fail to fulfil this role and it can bring great frustration to the women.

*The proof of legitimate authority is provision, protection and promotion.*
When my wife and I counsel couples, one of the first questions we ask is, where each of them falls in terms of their age amongst their siblings.

Our reason for this question is, because in most cases it affects peoples thinking and behaviour.

- The eldest child is always given the responsibility by the parents of looking after the younger ones. This develops a natural leadership within that child.
- The baby is used to being looked after and cared for and never takes responsibility.
- The middle child is caught between never getting leadership responsibility and also not receiving the attention of a baby. Most times these kids are the naughty ones, doing anything just to be seen by the parents. Which in most cases they are, but they don't think so. Many middle children will do anything for other people just to get acknowledgement.

If the husband was the eldest amongst his siblings and his wife was the youngest amongst hers, their marriage is well balanced. He is used to taking the lead and she is used to being looked after. When it is the other way around and the parent didn't teach the baby boy to lead, he will frustrate his wife, who was the eldest and she naturally takes the lead.

Women need affection like a man needs sex. Affection make her function well. The husband must love his wife and shower her with affection. When you speak to most women this is not about how much money he spends on her, although that is nice, it's about the quality time spent.  Many men do not see it that way and sacrifices his time working trying to please her, having no time for affection, as a man's pride is in his ability to provide. The woman feels dishonoured by his lack of affection.

**The curse God spoke over the man is: Cursed is the ground for thy sake; in sorrow thou eat of it all the days of thy life. (Genesis 3v17).**

God was telling the man you will work hard for little reward. A man's pride is in his ability to provide for his family. I have seen this frustration, where women get jobs quicker than men. It is said that women are more diligent in the work place, but they are not fighting the curse of the man. This however, is not an excuse for him to sit at home and not provide for his family.

You will find that women are better supporters of projects with their monies than men are, because the men feel they have worked too hard for little reward. Most men will tell you they don't earn enough.

Women, I am explaining this so that you can deal with your man with understanding. God has designed him to be your provider, but he is struggling with the very thing he has been designed for (the curse of toil and labour).

**Why a man needs a Pastor.**

Adam had communion with God every day in the garden. Out of this communion came the instructions from God and his assignment was clear. After the curse was spoken, man now had to work long hours and no longer had enough time for communion with God, so his assignment is not known. God in his mercy, sends him a pastor who spends time in the presence of God to get direction. When the pastor preaches on a Sunday what he got out of his communion with God, he gives the man direction and wisdom for his assignment.

Men, God expects of you to be a provider, protector and to take your wife into the purposes and plans God has for your lives.

- When you stay out of church and she must take the children, you have dishonoured her with your weak leadership.
- When she must get up to go work and you laying at home too lazy to work, you have dishonoured her.

- When you want her to treat you like a king, but you can't provide her with a castle, you have dishonoured her. When she has to become the

protector of the family, you have dishonoured her.
- When you don't give her the affection she needs to function well, you have dishonoured her.

The curses I have mentioned in this chapter, can be broken with wisdom and understanding. Being saved alone does not change it. I know many saved people who are struggling in these areas. They are being destroyed for lack of knowledge. Dr Murdock says," You will never have a marriage problem, the only problem you have is a wisdom problem.

*Choose today to live a life of honour within your marriage.*

# CHAPTER 11

## HONOUR TOWARDS OUR LEADERS IN GOVERNMENT

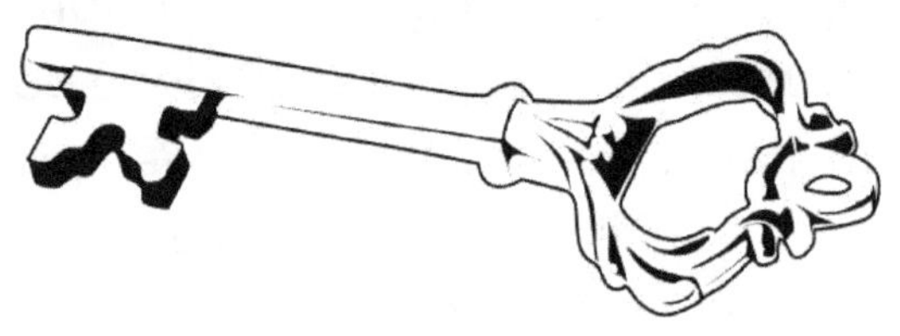

<u>Wisdom key:</u>

Honour has a fragrance...

just like dishonour has an odour

-    Ps Clint Ross

God expects of us to honour our government.

**Give to everyone what you owe them: Pay your taxes and government fees to those who collect them and give respect and honour to those who are in authority. Romans 13v7 (NLT)**

South Africa, the land that I love and grew up in, has a rich political history. One that for many years, I have not had much interest in while growing up. When I look back, I realise that my parents shielded us from getting involved in any political activities. My upbringing was during the apartheid era of our country and many of my friends at school fought that evil system.

My parents never wanted us as their children, to get involved in the fight against that system, as many young people lost their lives or were detained for it. I remember my brother Chris, going to university and coming back home with strong political opinions, as the students were a huge part of what they called, "The

Struggle." My parents did not appreciate much of his views, as anyone who spoke against the government was seen as a rebel.

In 1994 South Africa became a democratic country, and for the first time we could all vote. Many things were a first for us.

- Our first black president Mr Mandela
- We could go to any beach
- We could walk in any area or suburb
- Buy property in any area
- Get jobs that were previously only for the privileged minority etc.

 The country celebrated this new-found freedom and we were called the rainbow nation, because of our diverse racial groups. Surely now things are going to be much better, as we have the government we have been praying and fighting for. Many presidents have since come and gone and as I grew older, I realised that dishonouring authority had nothing to do with a system, but is rooted in the hearts of man.

As I'm writing this book, it is 2018 and our president has just been recalled from office. Being in office for almost 9 years, has seen him being mocked and criticized by many. New political party ruling, black president as we all prayed for, yet still continued dishonour from the people.

**What the Holy Spirit Kept Telling Me**

**...Honour the king. (1 Peter 2v17)**

When political parties run for elections, they are peers and should honour each other as such. However, the moment anyone is elected into the office of president, they become the authority and should then be honoured by all as such.

Our previous president Mr Zuma, had done many things that has caused people to frown on his leadership and within his last few days as president, every social media platform had videos and pictures of dishonour about him ... some of which I thought was quite funny and wanted to pass it on to my friends. A heavy conviction came over me every time the thought of passing it on, crossed my mind. The Holy Spirit said to me, *"You asked me to teach you honour. God is a leader in heaven and is passionate about every leader being honoured. He knows what it is like to have rebels rise up against Him in heaven."* It was like scales that fell off my eyes and I saw every leader in every environment as valuable. I could no longer laugh at a leader being mocked in any environment, because I know it grieves the Holy Spirit.

Are there things that leaders do that I disagree with? Yes for sure. My reactions to them has nothing to do with them, but everything to do with God's blessing upon my life.

One day when I heard of a man that was ordained into an office, I was very upset. I complained by some of my friends and said they were wrong to do this. Then the Holy Spirit asked me a question, *"Are you his authority?"* The answer was obvious, no. He then posed the following question, *"If a man's authority qualifies him for an office, why are you upset?"* Then He said, *"Whenever you see him you greet him by that title whether you believe in it or not. His leaders do and that is good enough for me."* I then realised that when a man has been ordained or holds a specific office, he is worthy of the honour due.

**Render therefore to all their dues: tribute to whom tribute is due; custom to whom custom; fear to whom fear; honour to whom honour. – (Romans 13v7)**

# CHAPTER 12

**BECOME A VESSEL OF HONOUR**

**7 Things You Can Do to Make People Feel Honoured**

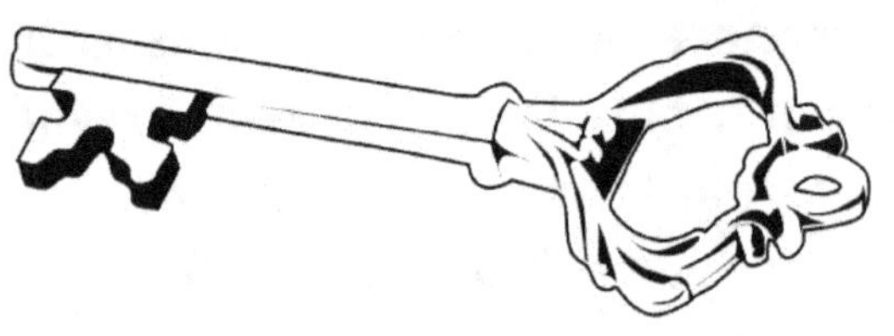

<u>Wisdom key:</u>

Honour qualifies you for rewards -

Ps Clint Ross

**But in a great house there are not only
vessels of gold and silver, but also of wood
and of earth; and some to honour, and
some to dishonour. If a man therefore
purge himself from these, he shall be a
vessel unto honour, sanctified, and meet
for the master's use, and prepared unto
every good work. (2 Timothy 2v20-21)**

A vessel of dishonour is not fit for the
master's use. You wonder why you are
struggling in life and cannot be blessed…
because you are a vessel of dishonour.

When you become a vessel of honour,
people want you in their environment and
are keen to show you favour.

Favour is when someone uses their gifts,
skills, influence, money etc. to help you
achieve your goals and dreams. There is a
difference between being loved and being
liked by people. People who love you won't
always show you favour, but people who
like you find ways to bless you. Think about
some of your family members, you love
them, but that does not mean you like them

enough to show them favour. Do you know how quickly I respond to people that I like?

***7 THINGS YOU CAN DO TO MAKE PEOPLE FEEL HONOURED***

1. *Honour the gift of time.*

**Ecclesiastes 3v1 To everything there is a season, and a time to every purpose under the heaven.**

Time is a gift from God to us that must be valued, if we want to see progress and increase in our lives. One of the biggest differences between the poor and the wealthy is the valuing of their time. Dr Murdock writes a great chapter on time in **The Law of Recognition.**

**Wisdom key:** Your respect for time is a prediction of your financial future. Dr Mike Murdock.

We all receive 24 hours in a day, the poor doesn't get less and the rich more. It is important that you learn to value your time and the time of others. People who don't value their own time, think nothing of wasting someone else's time.

Never go to anyone's house without calling them to confirm if it's a good time to come. When you go without confirming that you are coming, you expect of them to leave everything they're doing to make time for you. Some people have come to my house unannounced and expected of me to give them three hours of my day. They're sitting there talking a load of nonsense, and you must sit and look interested. Those days for me are over, my time is too valuable. I'm not saying that you must not have down time or play time, but it must be planned and confirmed with the people you want to spend it with. Your parents love you, but you visiting their house unannounced every time with your family, is going to cause frustration with them. I have seen this with my parents. I made it a habit of calling them and asking if it was a good time to visit.

When someone makes an appointment to see you, don't only give them a time to come ... also give them the time they must leave. Tell them, "I can see you from 10am to 12pm." If they arrive at 11am they only have one hour with you.

If you are running late for a meeting, it's important to phone and say that you will be late. The person waiting for you could then finish other things while waiting.

When you start to value your time, people might think you're a snob, but you cannot think like a peasant and expect to reach the palace. By managing my time, I am also working away my frustration of not completing the important tasks of my day.

Honour your time and the time of others, so that you don't lose the favour of access ... train yourself for your blessed future.

2.  *Honour the protocol of an environment*

Every environment has rules, spoken or unspoken. It is important for you to discover these rules that has been set by the authority of the environment. This is called honouring the protocol of the environment. Only the authority in that environment has the right to change the rules, unless he delegates it to someone else to do.

When you are visiting someone's home, make sure that you abide by the rules. I never allow people into my bedroom, but I have found at times, that people will enter my bedroom without my permission. The rules of my house do not allow that to happen. As a guest, you ask first before you enter any room in a home.

I have had pastors visiting me and as I walked into my study, I would find they have followed me there, without my permission. They then start looking through my books, asking if they can borrow it. I place a high value on my books and am offended with this type of behaviour. I then think twice before inviting them back to my house.

By honouring the protocol of an environment, you are also proving your honour towards the relationship.

I have seen many men with great gifting preach in churches, but are never invited back, because they could not honour the protocol of the environment.

I've just returned from a church that has two services on a Sunday morning, I was given a half an hour slot to preach in each service. The pastor asked me to please stick to the time, as this makes it easier for them to manage the crowds while changing services. I felt that I had much more to tell the people, but because of the rules of the house, I had to abide by the time allocated. After the second service, the pastor got up and said I am welcome back at any time, because I stuck to the time that was allocated to me.

I always teach my pastors and leaders, that when you are visiting a church, it is best to go and sit at the back and for them to invite you to the front. Rather than going to sit in front and them having to ask you to be seated elsewhere.

This applies to any environment, whether it be in your work place, at church, or in the home. Honouring the rules of an environment will create great favour, which gives you continuous access into that environment.

3.  Honouring Privacy

**Proverbs 11v13 A talebearer revealeth secrets: but he that is of a faithful spirit concealeth the matter.**

This one overlaps with the previous point of honouring an environment. However, not only honouring people's private space, but also what they share with you in private.

Be someone that can be trusted when private and confidential information is shared with you. This is rare and your value immediately increases, when people discover that you have this ability.

Honouring privacy is also knowing what questions to ask and what not to ask. You never ask people what they earn or have paid for their homes, whether they're renting it or bought it. This goes for their clothes, their cars, or any of their other possessions, unless they volunteer the information.

You also don't ask private questions about their family life, because you never know how sensitive situations can be.

I have seen how people were asked personal questions in public, that they refused to answer, and this created an unpleasant awkwardness for everyone in the room. Do not pry into other people's matters, this might not be your intent, but rather steer clear from creating an uncomfortable environment.

Honouring privacy puts you in a group of elite people, who will excel in high-level environments.

4.  Honouring Instructions.

**Proverbs 13v18 Poverty and shame shall be to him that refuseth instruction: but he that regardeth reproof shall be honoured.**

God in one sentence explains the cause of poverty, your unwillingness to follow an instruction. God has instructions throughout his word... your parents give instructions... so does your boss and your pastor.

One of the biggest differences in people, is their ability to follow an instruction correctly.

You create favour with any authority that does not have to repeat the same instruction twice. Dr Murdock believes that if your boss gives you the same instruction twice, you should be earning half of your salary. If he gives you the same instruction five times, you're a child and should be on an allowance.

I have given an instruction in our church on what to do with the money after the offering has been taken. Not too long ago, I returned from travelling for two weeks. When I came back, I observed that my instruction had been changed. Never change an instruction in any environment where you are not the final authority. Do not assume that you know what is good in the absence of your leader, by changing any rules that he has put in place. This counts in your work place, at church, at home etc. Follow the instructions given by your authority, until they decide when it should be changed.

One of the quickest ways to lose favour from authority, is by not following an instruction that they give you.

5.  Honouring Your Words

**Matthew 12v37 For by thy words thy shall be justified, and by thy words thou shall be condemned.**

*Are you a person of your word?*

*Can your word be honoured?*

*Can your word be trusted?*

*Or do you just say things without any meaning?*

I am learning that my words are valuable and that at all times, I should be conscious of what I am saying. Due to the fact that I love people, I can easily pay them a compliment, but I have also realised that at times I have been untruthful, wanting them to feel good. If you don't mean it, rather don't say it.

*God is big on words, He loved words so much he calls himself the Word.*

I have seen how easily people can tell others "I am praying for you" and all they did was think about them. Thinking about praying for someone, is not praying for someone. Hoping that things will go better for them, is also not praying for them. Let your words be true when you make statements.

When people know that you value your words and that you are truthful, it's easier for them to trust you.

6.  Honouring the Possessions of Others.

**Luke 16v12 if ye have not been faithful in that which is another man's, who shall give you that which is your own?**

**Luke chapter 16** speaks of a bad steward that was fired because he was unable to look after the possessions of another man.

If something does not belong to you and you are given the privilege of looking after it or using it, make sure you treat it better than you would your own possessions. This can be a car, a home, a business, even something as simple as clothing.

People have asked me to use of my possessions, gave it back and only when I wanted to use it again, I discovered it was broken. They don't have the decency to tell you that they damaged it. When I confronted some of these people, they would be angrier at me and make me feel like I'm being petty or am a liar.

My wife and I are very different in allowing people to use our possessions. I would easily give my car to someone else to drive, whereas my wife would not give her car to anyone else to drive. I have learnt that this has saved her from many unwanted situations with people we call friends.

Firstly, I would encourage you to not borrow other people's possessions. If they do ask you to look after it, make sure that you handle it with care, honesty and honour.

If a man has entrusted you to look after his business, make sure that you handle it frugally.

It is important that you honour the possessions of other people.

7.  Honouring Your Body.

**1 Corinthians 6vs16 What? know ye not that your body is the temple of the Holy Ghost which is in you, which ye have of God, and ye are not your own?**

This is something that I am only learning now and taking much more seriously in my life. When we are young, we don't consider our health much, but our bodies are to be treated with honour and respect.

I have seen how many people's lives have been shortened by them abusing their bodies with drugs, alcohol, cooldrinks and all kinds of bad food that we digest. This affects not only us, but also our loved ones. As we know the adverse effects that drugs and alcohol has had on our communities, as well as the illnesses that are caused by the food we digest. How our loved ones has to care for us or feel the heartache of losing us to death.

Dr Murdock has taught us that your decisions are more powerful than your prayers. If you have sugar diabetes and you're praying for healing, that prayer will be nullified if you finish a 2-litre coke afterwards. Your decisions must line up with your prayers.

Honour your body so that you can live long and fulfil the assignment that God has for your life.

*It is my prayer that you will become a vessel of honour.*

CLINT ROSS WITH DR MIKE MURDOCK
CLINT ROSS
CR
MINISTRIES
....HONOR WILL TAKE YOU FURTHER THAN YOUR FAITH /GIFT/ GENIUS /EDUCATION....

CLINT ROSS
WITH HIS FAMILY

HOUSE OF MERCY
THE WISDOM CENTER FORT WORTH TEXAS
RECONCILIATION MINISTRIES
ENON TABERNACLE BAPTIST CHURCH
NEW COVENANT CHRISTIAN CHURCH
JUDAH WORSHIP CENTRE
NEW COVENANT FELLOWSHIP - DURBAN
HONOUR
KING OF KINGS
ACTS MISSION CHURCH HERMANUS
THE LOVE CHURCH
GRACE MINISTRIES INTERNATIONAL
REVIVAL WORSHIP CENTRE
VICTORY CHURCH
SOWERS OF THE WORD CAPE TOWN
TABERNACLE OF PRAISE
OASIS FAMILY FELLOWSHIP
OUDTSHOORN COMMUNITY CHURCH
HOUSE OF GRACE RONGAI KENYA
CLINT ROSS PREACHING AT VARIOUS CHURCHES ALL OVER THE WORLD

# OUT PARTNERSHIP

I, Pastor Clint, love to be accessible to everyone and teach them the Wisdom of God. Covenant Partners help me in fulfilling the vision God has given me to pursue, proclaim and practice the Wisdom of God. No church is too big or too small for me to bless them. There are churches who needs my help and your seed of love into my ministry makes it possible for me to reach many more. If you have been blessed by this book, our Dr Mike Murdock School of Wisdom, through one of our services or special events, I would like to invite you to join me and be a partner in the change that God is bringing about in the lives of many. I hereby invite you to sow a seed into my ministry. Every seed is valuable, precious and appreciated.

Please find my ministry banking details below:

Account name: Clint Ross Ministries

Nedbank – Cheque account

Account no: 1073467295

Branch code: 198765

Swift code: (International transfers): NEDSZAJJ

Forward your contact details to info@theglobalwisdomcentre.co.za and become a Covenant Partner in prayer and financial support with Clint Ross Ministries today!